HYMNS

FOR

INFANT MINDS.

BY

THE AUTHORS

OF

" ORIGINAL POEMS," " RHYMES FOR THE NURSERY," &c.

——" We use great plainness of speech."——

SECOND EDITION.

LONDON:

PRINTED FOR T. CONDER, BUCKLERSBURY:
SOLD ALSO BY
DARTON, HARVEY, & CO., GRACECHURCH STREET; AND
CONDER & JONES, ST. PAUL'S CHURCHYARD.
1810.

Printed by George Ellerton, Johnson's Court, London.

ADVERTISEMENT

TO THE FIRST EDITION.

———

THE " Divine Songs " of Dr. Watts, so beautiful, and so universally admired, almost discourage, by their excellence, a similar attempt; and lead the way, where it appears temerity to follow. But as the narrow limits to which he confined himself excluded a number of useful subjects, the following Hymns, though with much diffidence, are presented to the Public. The most obvious and interesting topics were already engaged; but if it appear that this volume of HYMNS FOR INFANT MINDS fulfils its humble promise, and adapts evangelical truths to the wants and feelings of childhood, in language which it understands, further apology may not be required. It has been composed with a view to different ages and degrees of intelligence, but uniformly with the sacrifice of poetry to simplicity, wherever they stood opposed.

To some of the pieces the title of Hymns may not appear correctly applied; but for this inaccuracy the nature of the subjects will, it is hoped, apologize.

CONTENTS.

vii

BOOKS FOR YOUTH,

Sold by DARTON, HARVEY, *and* Co. *Gracechurch Street;
and* THOMAS CONDER, *Bucklersbury.*

ORIGINAL POEMS FOR INFANT MINDS. By several Young Persons. 2 vols. half bound. Price 3s.
" We have seldom seen a book, the title of which has so well corresponded with the contents. The poetry is very superior to what is usually found in books of this kind, and the moral tendency of the whole is excellent."—*Imperial Review.*

RHYMES FOR THE NURSERY. By the Authors of " Original Poems." Price 1s. 6d. half bound.
" We have not room for extracts, or could convince our readers, that the writers of these ' Rhymes' have better claims to the title of poets, than many who arrogate to themselves that high appellation."—*Critical Review.*

RURAL SCENES, or a Peep into the Country, for Good Children; illustrated by nearly 100 Cuts, with appropriate Descriptions in Prose and Verse. By the Authors of " Original Poems." Price 2s. 6d. neatly half bound.

CITY SCENES, or a Peep into London, for Good Children; with 103 Copper-plates. By the Authors of " Rural Scenes." Price 2s. 6d. half bound.

LIMED TWIGS, to catch Young Birds. By the Authors of " Original Poems." Price 2s. half bound.

The WEDDING AMONG THE FLOWERS; with Plates. By one of the Authors of " Original Poems." Price 1s.

CHRISTIAN PRUDENCE: consisting of Maxims and Proverbs, Divine and Moral, collected from the sacred Scriptures, the Writings of primitive Fathers, heathen Philosophers, and eminent Divines. 4th Edition, corrected and enlarged. Price 1s. in extra boards, or 10s. per Dozen.

HYMNS

FOR

INFANT MINDS,

&c. &c.

I.

A CHILD'S HYMN OF PRAISE.

I THANK the goodness and the grace
   Which on my birth have smil'd,
And made me, in these christian days,
   A happy English child.

I was not born, as thousands are,
   Where GOD was never known;
And taught to pray a useless pray'r,
   To blocks of wood and stone.

B

I was not born a little slave,
   To labour in the sun,
And wish I were but in the grave,
   And all my labour done!

I was not born without a home,
   Or in some broken shed;
A gipsy baby; taught to roam,
   And steal my daily bread.

My GOD, I thank thee, who hast plann'd
   A better lot for me,
And plac'd me in this happy land,
   And where I hear of thee.

II.

COMING TO JESUS.

JESUS, that condescending King,
Is pleas'd to hear when children sing,
And, while our feeble voices rise,
Will not the humble pray'r despise.

Then keep us, Lord, from ev'ry sin,
Which we can see and feel within;
And what we neither feel nor see,
Forgive, for all is known to thee.

We own there's nothing good in us,
To tempt thee to befriend us thus:
For sin and folly waste our days,
Our pray'rs are weak, and poor our praise:

Yet, Lord, we humbly venture nigh,
Because thou camest down to die:
And all the plea we dare to make
Is, " pardon, for thy mercy's sake."

III.

ABOUT GOD, WHO MADE THE SUN AND MOON.

Child.

I saw the glorious sun arise
    From yonder mountain grey;
And as he travell'd through the skies,
    The darkness fled away;

And all around me was so bright,
I wish'd it would be always light.

But when his shining course was done,
  The gentle moon drew nigh,
And stars came twinkling, one by one,
  Upon the shady sky.—
Who made the sun to shine so far,
The moon, and ev'ry twinkling star?

Mamma.

'Twas GOD, my child, who made them all,
  By his almighty hand:
He holds them, that they do not fall,
  And bids them move, or stand:
That glorious GOD, who lives afar,
In heav'n, beyond the highest star.

Child.

How very great that GOD must be,
  Who rolls them through the air!
Too high, Mamma, to notice me,
  Or listen to my pray'r!

I fear he will not condescend
To be a little infant's friend.

Mamma.
O yes, my love; for though he made
   Those wonders in the sky,
You never need to be afraid
   He should neglect your cry;
For, humble as a child may be,
A praying child he loves to see.

Behold the daisy where you tread,
   That useless little thing;
Behold the insects overhead,
   That gambol in the spring:
His goodness bids the daisy rise,
And ev'ry insect's want supplies:

And will he not descend to make
   A feeble child his care?
Yes! Jesus died for children's sake,
   And loves the youngest pray'r.—
God made the stars, and daisies too,
And watches over them and you.

IV.

FOR A CHILD WHO HAS BEEN VERY NAUGHTY.

Lord, I confess before thy face
    How naughty I have been:
Look down from heav'n, thy dwelling-place,
    And pardon this my sin.

Forgive my temper, Lord, I pray,
    My passion, and my pride;
The wicked words I dar'd to say,
    And wicked thoughts beside.

I cannot lay me down to rest
    In quiet, on my bed,
Until with shame I have confest
    The naughty things I said.

The Saviour answer'd not again,
    Nor spoke an angry word,
To all the scoffs of wicked men,
    Although he was their Lord!

7

And who am I, a sinful child,
  Such angry words to say !—
Make me as mild as he was mild,
  And take my pride away.

For Jesus' sake forgive my crime,
  And change this stubborn heart ;
And grant me grace, another time,
  To act a better part.

V.

"OUR FATHER, WHO ART IN HEAVEN."

Great God, and wilt thou condescend
To be my Father, and my Friend ?—
I a poor child, and thou so high,
The Lord of earth, and air, and sky !

Art thou my Father ?—Canst thou bear
To hear my poor, imperfect pray'r ;
Or stoop to listen to the praise
That such a little one can raise !

B 4

Art thou my Father?—Let me be
A meek, obedient child to thee;
And try, in word, and deed, and thought,
To serve and please thee as I ought.

Art thou my Father?—I'll depend
Upon the care of such a friend;
And only wish to do, and be,
Whatever seemeth good to thee.

Art thou my Father?—then, at last,
When all my days on earth are past,
Send down, and take me, in thy love,
To be thy better child, above.

VI.

"EARLY WILL I SEEK THEE."

Now that my journey's just begun,
　My road so little trod,
I'll come, before I further run,
　And give myself to GOD.

And, lest I should be ever led
　　Through sinful paths to stray,
I would at once begin to tread
　　In wisdom's pleasant way.

What sorrows may my steps attend
　　I never can foretel;
But if the Lord will be my friend,
　　I know that all is well.

If all my earthly friends should die,
　　And leave me mourning here;
Since God can hear the orphan's cry,
　　O what have I to fear!

If I am poor, He can supply
　　Who *has* my table spread;
Who feeds the ravens when they cry,
　　And fills his poor with bread.

If I am rich, He'll guard my heart,
　　Temptation to withstand;
And make me willing to impart
　　The bounties of his hand.

But, Lord, whatever grief or ill
   For me may be in store,
Make me submissive to thy will,
   And I would ask no more.

Attend me through my youthful way,
   Whatever be my lot;
And when I'm feeble, old, and grey,
   O Lord, forsake me not.

Then still, as seasons hasten by,
   I will for heaven prepare;
That God may take me when I die,
   To dwell for ever there.

VII.

ENCOURAGEMENT FOR LITTLE CHILDREN.

God is so good that he will hear
   Whenever children humbly pray:
He always lends a gracious ear
   To what the youngest child can say.

11

His own most holy Book declares
  He loves good little children still,
And that he listens to their prayers,
  Just as a tender father will.

He loves to hear an infant tongue
  Thank him for all his mercies giv'n;
And when by babes his praise is sung,
  Their cheerful songs are heard in heav'n.

Come then, dear children, trust his word,
  And seek him for your friend and guide ;
Your little voices will be heard,
  And you shall never be deny'd.

VIII.

THE BIBLE.

This is a precious book indeed!
Happy the child that loves to read !
'Tis God's own word, which he has giv'n
To shew our souls the way to heav'n !

It tells us how the world was made;
And how good men the Lord obey'd:
There his Commands are written, too,
To teach us what we ought to do.

It bids us all from sin to fly,
Because our souls can never die :
It points to heav'n, where angels dwell ;
And warns us to escape from hell.

But, what is more than all beside,
The Bible tells us JESUS died!—
This is its best, its chief intent,
To lead poor sinners to repent.

Be thankful, children, that you may
Read this good Bible every day :
'Tis GOD's own word, which he has giv'n
To shew your souls the way to heaven.

IX.

AGAINST WANDERING THOUGHTS.

WHEN daily I kneel down to pray,
  As I am taught to do,
GOD does not care for what I say,
  Unless I *feel* it too.

Yet foolish thoughts my heart beguile;
  And when I pray, or sing,
I'm often thinking, all the while,
  About some other thing.

Some idle play, or childish toy,
  Can send my thoughts abroad;
Though this should be my greatest joy,
  To love and seek the Lord.

Oh! let me never, never, dare
  To act the trifler's part;
Or think that God will hear a pray'r
  That comes not from my heart!

But if I make His ways my choice,
 As holy children do,
Then, while I seek him with my voice,
 My heart will love him too.

X.

"A BROKEN AND CONTRITE HEART, O GOD, THOU
WILT NOT DESPISE."

THOUGH GOD preserves me ev'ry hour,
 And feeds me day by day,
I know it is not in my pow'r
 His goodness to repay.

The poorest child, the greatest king,
 Alike must humbly own,
No worthy present they can bring
 To offer at his throne ;

For we, and all our treasures too,
 Are His who reigns above :—
Then is there nothing I can do,
 To prove my grateful love ?

A broken heart he'll not despise,
   For 'tis his chief delight :
This is a humble sacrifice,
   Well-pleasing in his sight.

Though treasures brought before his throne
   Would no acceptance find,
He kindly condescends to own
   A meek and lowly mind.

This is an off'ring we may bring
   However mean our store :
The poorest child, the greatest king,
   Can give him nothing more.

XI.

THE WAY TO FIND OUT PRIDE.

Pride, ugly Pride, sometimes is seen
By haughty looks, and lofty mien ;
But oft'ner it is found, that Pride
Loves deep within the heart to hide ;

And, while the looks are mild and fair,
It sits and does its mischief there.
  Now, if you really wish to find
If Pride is lurking in your mind,
Inquire if you can bear a slight,—
Or patiently give up your right.—
Can you submissively consent
To take reproof and punishment,
And feel no angry temper start,
In any corner of your heart?—
Can you with frankness own a crime,
And promise for another time?
Or say you've been in a mistake;
Nor try some poor excuse to make,
But freely own that it was wrong
To argue for your side so long?—
Flat contradiction can you bear,
When you are right, and know you are:
Nor flatly contradict again,
But wait, or modestly explain,
And tell your reasons one by one,
Nor think of triumph, when you've done?-
Can you, in business or in play,
Give up your wishes, or your way?—

Or do a thing against your will,
For somebody that's younger still ?—
And never try to overbear,
Or say a word that is not fair ?—
Does laughing at you, in a joke,
No anger, nor revenge, provoke ;
But can you laugh yourself, and be
As merry as the company ?—
Or, when you find that you could do
To them, as they have done to you,
Can you keep down the wicked thought,
And do exactly as you ought?

    Put all these questions to your heart,
And make it act an honest part,
And, when they've each been fairly try'd,
I think you'll own that you have pride :
Some one will suit you, as you go,
And force your heart to tell you so ;
But if they all should be denied,
Then—you're too proud to own your pride !

XII.

THE WAY TO CURE PRIDE.

Now I suppose, that, having try'd,
And found the secret of your pride,
You wish to drive it from your heart,
And learn to act a humbler part.

Well, are you sorry and sincere?—
I'll try to help you then, my dear.
And first, the best, the surest way,
Is to kneel down at once, and pray:
The lowly SAVIOUR will attend,
And strengthen you, and stand your friend.
Tell him the mischief that you find
For ever working in your mind;
And beg his pardon for the past,
And strength to overcome at last.—
But, then, you must not go your way,
And think it quite enough to pray:
That is but doing half your task;
For you must *watch* as well as *ask*.
You pray for strength, and that is right;
But, then, it must be strength to fight;—

For where's the use of being strong,
Unless you conquer what is wrong?
  Then look within:—ask every thought,
If it be humble as it ought.
Put out the smallest spark of pride
The very moment 'tis descried :
And do not stay to think it o'er,
For while you wait it blazes more.
If it should take you by surprise,
And beg you just to let it rise,
And promise not to keep you long,
Say, " *No;* the *smallest* pride is wrong."
And when there's something so amiss,
That Pride says, " Take offence at *this ;*"
Then, if you feel at all inclin'd
To brood upon it in your mind,
And think revengeful thoughts within,
And wish it were not wrong to sin,
O stop at once !—for if you dare
To wish for sin,—that sin is there !
'Twil. then be best to go and pray
That GOD would take your pride away :
Or if just then you cannot go,
Pray in your thoughts, and GOD will know:

And beg his mercy to impart
That best of gifts—a humble heart.

    Remember, too, that you must pray,
And watch, and labour, *every* day :
Nor think it wearisome or hard
To be *for ever* on your guard :
No ; every morning must begin
With resolutions not to sin ;
And every evening recollect
How much you've fail'd in this respect.
Ask, whether such a guilty heart
Should act a proud, or humble, part;
Or, as the SAVIOUR was so mild,
Inquire if pride becomes a child ?
And, when all other means are try'd,
Be humble, that you've so much pride !

XIII.

A MORNING HYMN.

My Father, I thank thee for sleep,
  For quiet and peaceable rest :

I thank thee for stooping to keep
  An infant from being distrest:
how can a poor little creature repay
by fatherly kindness by night and by day!

My voice would be lisping thy praise,
  My heart would repay thee with love :—
O teach me to walk in thy ways,
  And fit me to see thee above ;
For JESUS said, " Let little children come nigh;"
And he will not despise such an infant as I.

As long as thou seest it right
  That here upon earth I should stay,
I pray thee to guard me by night,
  And help me to serve thee by day ;
That when all the days of my life shall have
        pass'd,
I may worship thee better, in heaven, at last.

XIV.

AN EVENING HYMN.

Lord, I have pass'd another day,
  And come to thank thee for thy care;
Forgive my faults in work and play,
  And listen to my evening pray'r.

Thy favour gives me daily bread,
  And friends, who all my wants supply;
And safely now I rest my head,
  Preserv'd and guarded by thine eye.

Look down in pity, and forgive
  Whate'er I've said or done amiss;
And help me, ev'ry day I live,
  To serve thee better than in this.

Now, while I sleep, be pleas'd to take
  A helpless child beneath thy care;
And condescend, for Jesus' sake,
  To listen to my evening pray'r.

23

XV.

FOR A CHILD THAT FEELS IT HAS A WICKED HEART.

WHAT is there, Lord, a child can do,
  Who feels with guilt opprest?
There's evil, that I never knew
  Before, within my breast.

My thoughts are vain; my heart is hard;
  My temper apt to rise:
And when I seem upon my guard,
  It takes me by surprise.

Whene'er to thy Commands I turn,
  I find I've broken them ;
And in thy holy Scriptures learn,
  That GOD will sin condemn:

And yet, if I begin to pray,
  And lift my feeble cry,
Some thought of folly, or of play,
  Prevents me when I try.

On many Sabbaths, though I've heard
   Of JESUS and of heav'n,
I've scarcely listen'd to thy word,
   Or pray'd to be forgiv'n!

O look with pity in thine eye
   Upon a heart so hard:
Thou wilt not slight a feeble cry,
   Or shew it no regard;

The work I cannot undertake
   I leave to thee alone;
And pray thee, for thy mercy's sake,
   To change this heart of stone.

XVI.

AGAINST ANGER AND IMPATIENCE.

WHEN, for some little insult giv'n,
   My angry passions rise,
I'll think how JESUS came from heav'n,
   And bore his injuries.

He was insulted every day,
　Though all his words were kind;
But nothing men could do or say
　Disturb'd his heav'nly mind.

Not all the wicked scoffs he heard
　Against the truths he taught,
Excited one reviling word,
　Or one revengeful thought.

And when upon the cross he bled,
　With all his foes in view;
" Father, forgive their sin," he said;
　" They know not what they do."

Dear Jesus, may I learn of thee
　My temper to amend;—
But speak that pardoning word for me
　Whenever I offend.

XVII.

"TURN OFF MINE EYES FROM BEHOLDING VANITY."

Lord, hear a sinful child complain,
Whose little heart is very vain—
   And folly dwells within:
What is it—for thine eye can see—
That is so very dear to me;
That steals my thoughts away from thee,
   And leads me into sin?

Whatever gives me most delight,
If 'tis offensive in thy sight,
   I would no more pursue:—
Since nothing can be good for me,
However pleasant it may be,
That is displeasing, Lord, to thee,
   May I dislike it too.

When I attempt to read or pray,
Some folly leads my heart astray,
   And sends my thoughts abroad :—

How happy are the saints in bliss,
Who love no sinful world like this,
But all their joy and glory is
   To serve and praise the Lord!

These trifling pleasures here below—
I wonder why I love them so;
   They cannot make me blest:
O that to love my GOD might be
The greatest happiness to me!
And may he give me grace to see
   That this is not my rest!

XVIII.

FOR A VERY LITTLE CHILD.

O THAT it were my chief delight
   To do the things I ought!—
Then let me try with all my might
   To mind what I am taught.

c 2

Wherever I am told to go,
  I'll cheerfully obey;
Nor will I mind it much, although
  I leave a pretty play.

When I am bid, I'll freely bring
  Whatever I have got;
And never touch a pretty thing,
  If Mother tells me not.

When she permits me, I may tell
  About my little toys;
But if she's busy or unwell,
  I must not make a noise.

And when I learn my hymns to say,
  And work, and read, and spell,
I will not think about my play,
  But try and do it well:

For God looks down from heav'n on high
  Our actions to behold;
And he is pleas'd when children try
  To do as they are told.

XIX.

ON ATTENDING PUBLIC WORSHIP.

When to the house of God we go,
　To hear his word, and sing his love,
We ought to worship him below,
　Like all the saints in heaven above.

They stand before his presence now,
　And praise him better far than we,
Who only at his footstool bow,
　And love him, though we cannot see.

But God is present every-where,
　And watches all our thoughts and ways;
He sees who humbly join in pray'r,
　And who sincerely sing his praise.

And he the triflers, too, can see,
　Who only *seem* to take a part:
They move the lip, and bend the knee,
　But do not seek him with the heart.

c 3

O may we never trifle so,
  Nor lose the days our GOD has giv'n;
But learn, by Sabbaths here below,
  To spend Eternity in heav'n!

XX.

A CHILD'S HUMBLE CONFESSION AND PRAYER.

A SINNER, Lord, behold I stand;
  In thought, and word, and deed!—
But JESUS sits at thy right hand,
  For such to intercede.

From early infancy, I know,
  A rebel I have been,
And daily, as I older grow,
  I fear I grow in sin:—

But GOD can change this evil heart,
  And give a holy mind,
And his own heav'nly grace impart,
  Which those who seek shall find.

To heav'n can reach the softest word—
 A child's repenting prayer—
For tears are seen, and sighs are heard,
 And thoughts regarded, there.

Then let me all my sins confess,
 And pardoning grace implore ;
That I may love my follies less,
 And love my SAVIOUR more.

XXI.

ABOUT DYING.

Child.

TELL me, Mamma, if I must die
One day, as little baby died ;
And look so very pale, and lie
Down in the pit-hole, by its side ?

Shall I leave dear Papa and you,
And never see you any more ;
Tell me, Mamma, if this is true :
I did not know it was before.

Mamma.

'Tis true, my love, that you must die;
  The God who made you, says you must;
And every one of us shall lie,
  Like the dear baby, in the dust.

These hands, and feet, and busy head,
  Shall waste and crumble quite away:
But though your body shall be dead,
  There is a part which can't decay:

That which now thinks within your heart,
  And made you ask if you must die,
That is your soul—the better part—
  Which God has made to live on high.

Those who have lov'd him here below,
  And pray'd to have their sins forgiv'n,
And done his holy will, shall go,
  Like happy angels, up to heav'n:

So, while their bodies moulder here,
  Their souls with God himself shall dwell;
But always recollect, my dear,
  That wicked people go to hell.

There the good God shall never smile,
Nor give them one reviving look;
For since they chose to be so vile,
He leaves them to the way they took.

XXII.

"THOU, GOD, SEEST ME."

AMONG the deepest shades of night
  Can there be one who sees my way?
Yes;—GOD is like a shining light,
  That turns the darkness into day.

When ev'ry eye around me sleeps,
  May I not sin without controul?
No; for a constant watch He keeps,
  On ev'ry thought of ev'ry soul.

If I could find some cave unknown,
  Where human feet had never trod,
Yet there I could not be alone;
  On every side there would be GOD;

He smiles in heaven; He frowns to hell;
   He fills the air, the earth, the sea :—
I *must* within his presence dwell;
   I *cannot* from his anger flee.—

Yet I may flee—he shews me where;
   Tells me to JESUS CHRIST to fly :
And while he sees me weeping there,
   There's only mercy in his eye.

XXIII.

TO A LITTLE SISTER, ON HER BIRTH-DAY.

My love, I meet this happy day
   With pleasure, and with pain :
I wish to learn your future way,
   But know the wish is vain.

A journey which can never end
   You have but just begun;
And hand in hand with many a friend
   This little way have run :

But friends, my love, how vain are they !
   For one infected breath
May snatch the tenderest away,
   And seal them up in death.

Then whither should my darling fly ?
   In whom may she confide ?—
There is a Friend above the sky,
   Who waits to be her guide.

His eye the path of life can see,
   And has as clear a view
Of hills and valleys yet to be,
   As what are past to you.

He knows the point, the very spot,
   Where each of us shall fall ;
And whose shall be the earliest lot,
   And whose the last of all.

Dear cherish'd child ! if *you* should have
   To travel far alone,
And weep by turns at many a grave,
   Before you reach your own,

May He, who bade you weep, be nigh
  To wipe away your tears,
And point you to a world on high,
  Beyond these mournful years!

Yet, if it be his holy will,
  I pray that hand in hand
We *all* may travel many a hill
  Of this the pilgrim's land;

With Zion's shining gate in view,
  Through ev'ry danger rise;
And form a family anew,
  Unbroken, in the skies.

XXIV.

SIN MAKES GOD ANGRY.

How kind, in all his works and ways,
  Must our Creator be!
I learn a lesson of his praise
  From every thing I see.

Ten thousand creatures by his hand
   Were brought to life at first :
His skill their different natures plann'd,
   And made them from the dust :

He condescends to do them good,
   And pities when they cry ;
For all their wants are understood
   By his attentive eye.

And can so kind a Father frown ?
   Will he, who stoops to care
For little sparrows falling down,
   Despise an infant's pray'r ?

No ; he regards the feeblest cry :
   'Tis only when we sin
He puts the smile of mercy by,
   And lets his frown begin.

'Tis sin that grieves his holy mind,
   And makes his anger rise ;
And sinners old or young shall find
   No favour in his eyes.

But, when the broken spirit burns,
   And would from sin depart,
The GOD of mercy never spurns
   That broken, humble heart.

XXV.

" JESUS CHRIST CAME INTO THE WORLD TO SAVE
SINNERS."

Lo, at noon 'tis sudden night !
   Darkness covers all the day !
Rocks are rending at the sight !——
   Children, can you tell me why ?
What can all these wonders be ?
—JESUS dies at Calvary !

Stretch'd upon the cross, behold
   How his tender limbs are torn !
For a royal crown of gold,
   They have made him one of thorn !
Cruel hands, that dare to bind
Thorns upon a brow so kind !

See! the blood is falling fast
  From his forehead and his side!
Listen! he has breath'd his last!
  With a mighty groan he died!—
Children, shall I tell you why
Jesus condescends to die?

He, who was a King above,
  Left his kingdom for a grave,
Out of pity and of love,
  That the guilty he might save!
Down to this sad world he flew,
For such little ones as you!

You were wretched, weak, and vile;
  You deserv'd his holy frown;
But he saw you with a smile,
  And to save you hasten'd down.—
Listen, children;—this is why
Jesus condescends to die.

Come then, children, come and see;
  Lift your little hands to pray:
D 2

" Blessed Jesus, pardon me,
   " Help a guilty infant," say ;
" Since it was for such as I
" Thou didst condescend to die."

XXVI.

" JESUS SAID, SUFFER LITTLE CHILDREN TO COM
UNTO ME."

As infants once to Christ were brought,
   That he might bless them there,
So now we little children ought
   To seek the same by pray'r.

For when their feeble hands were spread,
   And bent each infant knee,
" Forbid them not," the Saviour said ;
   And so he says for me.

Though now he is not here below,
   But on his heav'nly hill,
To him may little children go,
   And seek a blessing still.

Well pleas'd that little flock to see,
  The Saviour kindly smil'd:
Oh, then, he will not frown on me
  Because I am a child.

For as so many years ago
  Poor babes his pity drew,
I'm sure he will not let me go
  Without a blessing too.

Then while, this favour to implore,
  My little hands are spread,
Do thou thy sacred blessing pour,
  Dear Jesus, on my head.

XXVII.

LOVE AND DUTY TO PARENTS.

My Father, my Mother, I know
  I cannot your kindness repay;
But I hope, that, as older I grow,
  I shall learn your commands to obey.

You lov'd me before I could tell
    Who it was that so tenderly smil'd;
But now, that I know it so well,
    I *should* be a dutiful child.

I am sorry that ever I should
    Be naughty, and give you a pain;
I hope I shall learn to be good,
    And so never grieve you again.

But, for fear that I ever should dare
    From all your commands to depart,
Whenever I'm saying my pray'r
    I'll ask for a dutiful heart.

XXVIII.

THE DAY OF LIFE.

THE morning hours of cheerful light,
    Of all the day are best;
But as they speed their hasty flight,
If ev'ry hour is spent aright,
We sweetly sink to sleep at night,
    And pleasant is our rest.

And life is like a summer's day,
　　It seems so quickly past:
Youth is the morning bright and gay,
And if 'tis spent in wisdom's way,
We meet old age without dismay,
　　And death is sweet at last.

XXIX.

THE LITTLE PILGRIM.

THERE is a path that leads to GOD—
　　All others go astray—
Narrow, but pleasant, is the road;
　　And Christians love the way.

It leads straight through this world of sin;
　　And dangers must be past;
But those who boldly walk therein
　　Will come to heav'n at last,

How shall an infant pilgrim dare
　　This dangerous path to tread?

For on the way is many a snare
  For youthful trav'llers spread;

While the broad road where thousands go,
  Lies near, and opens fair :
And many turn aside I know,
  To walk with sinners there.

But, lest my feeble steps should slide,
  Or wander from thy way,
Lord, condescend to be my guide,
  And I shall never stray.

Then I may go without alarm,
  And trust his word of old ;—
" The lambs he'll gather with his arm,
  " And lead them to the fold."

Thus I may safely venture through,
  Beneath my Shepherd's care ;
And keep the gate of heav'n in view,
  Till I shall enter there.

XXX.

AN EVENING HYMN FOR A LITTLE FAMILY.

Now condescend, Almighty King,
  To bless this little throng;
And kindly listen while we sing
  Our pleasant ev'ning song.

We come to own the Pow'r divine
  That watches o'er our days;
For this our feeble voices join
  In hymns of cheerful praise.

Before thy sacred footstool see
  We bend in humble pray'r,
A happy little family,
  To ask thy tender care.

May we in safety sleep to-night,
  From every danger free;
Because the darkness and the light
  Are both alike to thee.

And when the rising sun displays
   His cheerful beams abroad,
Then shall our morning hymn of praise
   Declare thy goodness, LORD.

Brothers and sisters, hand in hand,
   Our lips together move ;
Then smile upon this little band,
   And join our hearts in love.

XXXI.

A CHILD'S LAMENTATION FOR THE DEATH OF A DEAR MOTHER.

A POOR afflicted child, I kneel
   Before my heav'nly Father's seat,
To tell him all the grief I feel,
   And spread my sorrows at his feet.

Yet I must weep: I cannot stay
   These tears, that trickle while I bend,
Since thou art pleas'd to take away
   So dear, so very dear a friend.

And now I recollect with pain
   The many times I griev'd her sore;
Oh! if she would but come again,
   I think I'd vex her so no more.

How I would watch her gentle eye!
   'Twould be my play to do her will!
And she should never have to sigh
   Again, for my behaving ill!

But since she's gone so far away,
   And cannot profit by my pains,
Let me this child-like duty pay
   To that dear parent who remains:

Let me console his broken heart,
   And be his comfort, by my care;
That when at last we come to part,
   I may not have *such* grief to bear.

XXXII.

FOR SABBATH EVENING.

WE'VE pass'd another Sabbath day,
   And heard of JESUS and of heav'n:
We thank thee for thy word, and pray
   That this day's sins may be forgiv'n.

Forgive our inattention, Lord,
   Our looks and thoughts that went astray
Forgive our carelessness abroad;
   At home, our idleness and play.

May all we heard and understood
   Be well remember'd through the week
And help to make us wise and good,
   More humble, diligent, and meek.

'Bless our good minister, we pray,
   Who loves to see a child attend,
And let us honour and obey
   The words of such a holy friend.

So, when our lives are finish'd here,
   And days and Sabbaths shall be o'er,
May we along with him appear,
   To serve and love thee evermore.

XXXIII.

TIME AND ETERNITY.

How long, sometimes, a day appears!
   And weeks, how long are they!
Months move as slow as if the years
   Would never pass away.

It seems a long, long time ago
   That I was taught to read;
And since I was a babe, I know
   'Tis very long indeed.

But even years are passing by,
   And soon must all be gone;
For day by day, as minutes fly,
   Eternity comes on.

Days, months, and years must have an end ;
    Eternity has none ;
'Twill always have as long to spend
    As when it first begun !

Great GOD ! an infant cannot tell
    How such a thing can be ;
I only pray that I may dwell
    That long, long time with thee.

XXXIV.

AGAINST YIELDING TO TEMPTATION.

My love, you have met with a trial to-day,
    Which I hop'd to have seen you oppose ;
But, alas ! in a moment your temper gave way,
    And the pride of your bosom arose.

I saw the temptation, and trembled, for fear
    Your good resolutions should fall :
And soon, by your eye, and your colour, my dear,
    I found you had broken them all.

O, why did you suffer this troublesome sin
   To rise in your bosom again?
And when you perceiv'd it already within,
   O why did you let it remain?

As soon as temptation is put in your way,
   And passion is ready to start,
'Tis then you must try to subdue it, and pray
   For courage to bid it depart.

But now you can only with sorrow implore
   That Jesus would pardon your sin;
Would help you to watch for your enemy more,
   And put a new temper within.

XXXV.

THE DAY OF JUDGMENT.

How dreadful, Lord, will be the day,
   When all the tribes of dead shall rise;
And those who dar'd to disobey
   Be dragg'd before thine angry eyes!

The wicked child, who often heard
 His pious parents speak of Thee,
And fled from ev'ry serious word,
 Shall not be able then to flee.

No: he shall see them burst the tomb,
 And rise, and leave him trembling there,
To hear his everlasting doom,
 With shame, and terror, and despair.

Whilst they appear at thy right hand,
 With saints and angels round the throne;
He, a poor guilty wretch, shall stand,
 And hear thy dreadful wrath alone!

No parent, then, shall bid him pray
 To Him, who *now* the sinner hears;
For CHRIST himself shall turn away,
 And shew no pity to his tears.

Great GOD! I tremble at the thought;
 And at thy feet for mercy bend,
That, when to judgment I am brought,
 The Judge himself may be my friend.

XXXVI.

CONSCIENCE.

When a foolish thought within
　Tries to take us in a snare,
Conscience tells us " It is sin,"
　And entreats us to beware.

If in something we transgress,
　And are tempted to deny,
Conscience says, " Your fault confess ;
　" Do not dare to tell a lie."

In the morning, when we rise,
　And would fain omit to pray,
" Child, consider," Conscience cries ;
　" Should not God be sought to-day ? "

When, within his holy walls,
　Far abroad our thoughts we send.
Conscience often loudly calls,
　And entreats us to attend.

When our angry passions rise,
　　Tempting to revenge an ill ;
" Now subdue it," Conscience cries ;
　　" Do command your temper still."

Thus, without our will or choice,
　　This good monitor within,
With a secret, gentle voice
　　Warns us to beware of sin.

But if we should disregard,
　　While this friendly voice would call,
Conscience soon will grow so hard,
　　That it will not speak at all.

XXXVII.

" THOUGH THE LORD BE HIGH, YET HATH HE
RESPECT UNTO THE LOWLY."

WHERE is the high and lofty Oné ?
　　His dwelling is afar ;
He lives beyond the blazing sun,
　　And ev'ry distant star.

But God, whom thousand worlds obey,
   Descends to earthly ground,
And dwells in cottages of clay,
   If there his saints are found.

Is not the heav'n of heav'ns his own?
   Yes—he is Lord of all ;—
And there, before his awful throne,
   The saints and angels fall.

But, little child, with joy attend ;
   For if you love him too,
This mighty God will condescend
   To come and dwell with you.

XXXVIII.

FOR CHILDREN AT A SUNDAY SCHOOL.

Lord, may a few poor children raise
To thee a hymn of humble praise?
'Tis by thy great compassion we
Are taught to love and worship thee.

What wicked children we have been!
Alas! how soon we learn'd to sin!
But *now* we learn to read and pray,
And not to break the Sabbath-day.

How condescending GOD must be,
To love such little ones as we!
He saw our sin with angry frown,
And yet he look'd with pity down.

O if we should again begin
To grieve our GOD, and turn to sin,
And let our guilty passions loose,
We now shall be without excuse.

Remember, LORD, we are but dust;
'Tis to thy grace alone we trust;
Do thou instruct and guide us still,
That we may ne'er forget thy will.

XXXIX.

A MINUTE.

A MINUTE, how soon it is flown!
  And yet how important it is!
GOD calls ev'ry moment his own,
  For all our existence is his;
And though we may waste them in folly and play,
He notices each that we squander away.

Why should we a minute despise
  Because it so quickly is o'er?
We know that it rapidly flies,
  And therefore should prize it the more:
Another, indeed, may appear in its stead,
But that precious minute for ever is fled.

'Tis easy to squander our years
  In idleness, folly, and strife;
But, oh! no repentance or tears
  Can bring back one moment of life;
But time, if well spent, and improv'd as it goes,
Will render life pleasant, and peaceful its close.

And when all the minutes are past,
   Which GOD for our portion has giv'n,
We shall cheerfully welcome the last,
   If it safely conduct us to heav'n.
And O may we all the necessity see,
Not knowing how near our last minute may be!

XL.

A CHILD'S GRAVE.

WHAT is this little grassy mound,
   Where pretty daisies bloom?
What is there lying under ground?—
   —It is an infant's tomb.

Alas, poor baby, did it die?
   How dismal that must be!
To bid this pretty world good-bye
   Seems very sad to me.—

—Silence, my child; for could we hear
   This happy baby's voice,
We should not drop another tear,
   But triumph and rejoice:

" O do not ever weep for me,"
  The happy soul would say ;
" Nor grieve, dear child, that I am free
  " From that poor sleeping clay.

" Mourn not because my feeble breath
  " Was stopp'd as soon as giv'n:
" There's nothing terrible in death
  " To those who come to heav'n.

" No sin, no sorrow, no complaints,
  " My pleasures here destroy:
" I live with GOD and all his saints,
  " And endless is our joy.

" While, with the spirits of the just,
  " My SAVIOUR I adore,
" I smile upon my sleeping dust,
  " That now can weep no more."

XLI.

A CHILD'S PRAYER IN SICKNESS.

SINCE, mighty GOD, my health, and ease,
    And life, belong to thee,
I might not murmur, shouldst thou please
    To take them all from me.

Thou hast a right to use thy rod,
    Which I should meekly bear;
And yet I may entreat that GOD
    A sinful child would spare.

I own the comforts I possess,
    And thank thy care of me,
While thousands languish in distress,
    And pine in poverty:

Yet look in pity on my pain;
    My little strength restore;
And grant me life and health again,
    To serve thee evermore.

XLII.

A HYMN OF PRAISE FOR RECOVERY.

Lord, thou hast heard my humble voice,
  For all my pains depart:
O grant that I may now rejoice
  With thankfulness of heart.

Many have died as young as I,
  Though nurs'd with equal care;
But God in pity heard my cry,
  And has been pleas'd to spare.

Let me improve the years, or days,
  Thy mercy lends me here;
And shew my gratitude and praise,
  By living in thy fear.

The kindness that my friends have shown,
  O teach me to repay,
By double kindness of my own,
  In ev'ry future day.

And, lest I need thy rod again,
  I pray thee to impart,
As long as health or life remain,
  A thankful, humble heart.

E

XLIII.

FOR A VERY LITTLE CHILD, IN SICKNESS.

ALMIGHTY GOD, I'm very ill,
But cure me, if it be thy will;
For thou canst take away my pain,
And make me strong and well again.

Let me be patient every day,
And mind what those who nurse me say;
And grant that all I have to take
May do me good,—for JESUS' sake.

XLIV.

FOR A VERY LITTLE CHILD, UPON GETTING WELI

I THANK the LORD, who lives on high:
He heard an infant pray,
And cur'd me, that I should not die,
And took my pains away.

O let me thank and love thee too,
   As long as I shall live;
And every naughty thing I do,
   I pray thee to forgive.

XLV.

FOR A DYING CHILD.

My Heav'nly Father, I confess
   That all thy ways are just,
Although I faint with sore distress,
   And now draw near the dust.

How soon my health and strength are fled!
   And life is nearly past!
O smile upon my dying bed,
   And love me to the last.

Once did the blessed Saviour cry,
   " Let little children come :"
On this kind word I would rely,
   Since I am going home.

O take this guilty soul of mine,
  That now will soon be gone,
And wash it clean, and make it shine,
  With heav'nly garments on.

Be pleas'd to grant me easy death,
  If 'tis thy holy will,
And bid the struggles of my breath
  And all my pains be still.

Now, Lord, in heav'n hear my pray'r;
  Accept my dying praise;
And let me quickly meet thee there,
  A better song to raise.

XLVI.

PRAISE FOR DAILY MERCIES.

Lord, I would own thy tender care
  And all thy love to me;
The food I eat, the clothes I wear,
  Are all bestow'd by thee.

'Tis thou preservest me from death
   And dangers every hour:
I cannot draw another breath
   Unless thou give me pow'r.

Kind angels guard me ev'ry night,
   As round my bed they stay;
Nor am I absent from thy sight
   In darkness, or by day.

My health, and friends, and parents dear,
   To me by GOD are giv'n,
I have not any blessing here
   But what is sent from Heav'n.

Such goodness, LORD, and constant care,
   A child can ne'er repay;
But may it be my daily pray'r
   To love thee and obey.

XLVII.

THE EXAMPLE OF CHRIST.

Jesus Christ, my Lord and Saviour,
   Once became a child like me:
O that in my whole behaviour
   He my pattern still might be

All my nature is unholy;
   Pride and passion dwell within:
But the Lord was meek and lowly,
   And was never known to sin.

While I'm often vainly trying
   Some new pleasure to possess,
He was always self-denying,
   Patient in his worst distress.

Lord, assist a feeble creature;
   Guide me by thy word of truth;
Condescend to be my teacher
   Through my childhood and my youth.

Often I shall be forgetful
   Of the lessons thou hast taught,
Idle, passionate, and fretful,
   Or indulging foolish thought.

Then permit me not to harden
   In my sin, and be content;
But bestow a gracious pardon,
   And assist me to repent.

XLVIII.

SUMMER AND WINTER.

When sweet summer flowers appear,
We wish that they always would last;
But Winter must shortly be here,
To sweep them away with his blast:
Spring, summer, and autumn still hasten away;
The roses must fade, and the blossoms decay.

Like winter, old age will be found;
All stripp'd of our blossoms and fruit,

We still may remain in the ground,
Though nothing be left but the root:
And wither'd and bare we must ever remain,
For spring will not cover our branches again.

Then let us, since time's on the wing,
And death and eternity near,
Endeavour, while yet in our spring,
To prepare for the end of the year;
That we may not look back with remorse and
dismay,
To think how this season was wasted away.

And then, when the summer is gone,
Our youth and maturity past,
Old age will come pleasantly on,
And bring us to glory at last;
Nor shall we reflect with a sigh or a tear
On any gay season of happiness here.

In heaven no winter they know
To wither their pleasures away;
The plants that in Paradise grow
Shall blossom, but never decay:

Then for these fading pleasures no longer we'll
    care,
But hope we shall spend an eternity there.

XLIX.

LOVE TO JESUS.

WHEN JESUS CHRIST was here below,
  And spread his works of love abroad,
If I had liv'd so long ago,
  I think I should have lov'd the LORD.

JESUS, who was so very kind,
  Who came to pardon sinful men,
Who heal'd the sick, and cur'd the blind—
  O! must I not have lov'd him then?

But where is JESUS?—is he dead?
  O no! he lives in heav'n above;
" And blest are they," the SAVIOUR said,
  " Who, though they have not seen me, love."

He sees us, from his throne on high,
  As well as when on earth he dwelt;
And when to him poor children cry,
  He feels such love as then he felt.

And if the LORD will grant me grace,
  Much I will love him, and adore;
But when in heav'n I see his face,
  'Twill be my joy to love him more.

L.

GOD EVERY WHERE.

GOD made the world—in ev'ry land
  His love and power abound:
All are protected by his hand
  As well as British ground.

The Indian hut, and English cot,
  Alike his care must own,
Though savage nations know him not,
  But worship wood and stone.

He sees and governs distant lands,
  And constant bounty pours,
From wild Arabia's burning sands
  To Lapland's frozen shores.

In forest shades, and silent plains,
  Where feet have never trod,
There in majestic power he reigns,
  An ever-present GOD.

All the inhabitants of earth
  Who dwell beneath the sun,
Of diff'rent nations, name, and birth,
  He knows them every one.

Alike the rich and poor are known,
  The polish'd, and the wild;
He sees the king upon the throne,
  And every little child.

While he regards the wise and fair.
  The noble and the brave,
He listens to the beggar's pray'r,
  And the poor Negro slave.

He knows the worthy from the vile,
  And sends his mercy down :
None are too mean to share his smile,
  Or to provoke his frown.

Great God ! and since thy piercing eye
  My inmost heart can see,
Teach me from every sin to fly,
  And turn that heart to thee.

LI.

"THOUGH HE WAS RICH, YET FOR OUR SAKES, HE
BECAME POOR."

Jesus was once despis'd and low,
  A stranger, and distress'd ;
Without a home to which to go,
  A pillow where to rest :

Now, on a high majestic seat
  He reigns above the sky ;
And angels worship at his feet ;
  Or at his bidding fly.

Once he was bound with prickly thorns,
　And scoff'd at in his pain ;
Now a bright crown his head adorns,
　And he is King again.

But what a condescending King !
　Who, though he reigns so high,
Is pleas'd when little children sing,
　And listens to their cry :

He sees them from his heav'nly throne,
　He watches all their ways,
And stoops to notice for his own
　The youngest child that prays.

LII.

FOR A CHILD THAT IS SORRY FOR A FAULT.

Lord, I have dar'd to disobey
　My friends on earth, and thee in heav'n ;
O help me now to come and pray,
　For Jesus' sake, to be forgiv'n.

F

I cannot say I did not know,
   For I've been taught thy holy will;
And while my conscience told me so,
   And bade me stop, I did it still.

But thou wast there to see my crime,
   And write it in thy judgment-book.—
O make me fear, another time,
   A sinful thought, or word, or look.

Forgive me, Lord; forgive, I pray,
   This naughty thing that I have done;
And take my sinful heart away,
   And make me holy, like thy Son.

LIII.

INSTRUCTION FROM THE HEAVENS.

Stars, that on your wond'rous way
   Travel through the ev'ning sky,
Is there nothing you can say
   To such a little child as I?

Tell me, for I long to know,
Who has made you sparkle so?

Yes, methinks I hear you say,
  " Child of mortal race, attend,
While we run our wond'rous way ;
  Listen ; we would be your friend ;
Teaching you that Name Divine,
By whose mighty word we shine.

Child, as truly as we roll
  Through the dark and distant sky,
You have an immortal soul,
  Born to live when we shall die :
Suns and planets pass away ;
Spirits never can decay.

When some thousand years, at most,
  All their little time have spent,
One by one our sparkling host
  Shall forsake the firmament :
We shall from our glory fall;
You must live beyond us all.

Yes,—and GOD, who bade us roll,
 GOD, who hung us in the sky,
Stoops to watch an infant's soul
 With a condescending eye ;
And esteems it dearer far,
More in value, than a star !

O then, while your breath is giv'n,
 Pour it out in fervent pray'r,
And beseech the GOD of heav'n
 To receive your spirit there ;
Like a living star to blaze
Ever to your SAVIOUR's praise."

LIV.

CHILDREN ENCOURAGED TO SEEK THE LORD.

SHALL I presume to venture near
 A GOD so just and true ?
Or, sinful as I am, appear
 Before his piercing view ?

How oft I grieve his holy eye,
  And break his righteous law ;
And think some thought of vanity
  With ev'ry breath I draw !

Yet, Lord, a sinful child may turn
  To wisdom's pleasant ways ;
For JESUS' sake, thou wilt not spurn
  My feeble pray'r and praise.

He died, that sinners, such as I,
  May have their sins forgiv'n;
He died, that sinners, when they die,
  May live with him in heav'n.

It is for this I come to pray,
  And on his grace depend,
That even at the Judgment-day
  The Lord may be my friend.

LV.

UPON LIFE.

Lord, what is life ?—'Tis like a flow'r,
   That blossoms, and is gone :
We see it flourish for an hour,
   With all its beauty on ;
But Death comes, like a wintry day,
And cuts the pretty flow'r away.

Lord, what is life ?—'Tis like the bow
   That glistens in the sky :
We love to see its colours glow ;
   But while we look, they die :
Life fails as soon : to-day, 'tis here ;
To-night, perhaps, 'twill disappear.

Six thousand years have pass'd away
   Since life began at first,
And millions, once alive and gay,
   Are dead, and in the dust ;
For Life, in all its health and pride,
Has Death still waiting at its side.

And yet, this short, uncertain space
  So foolishly we prize,
That heav'n, that lasting dwelling-place,
  Seems nothing in our eyes!
The worlds of sorrow and of bliss
We disregard, compar'd with this!

Lord, what is life?—If spent with thee,
  In duty, praise, and pray'r,
However long or short it be,
  We need but little care;
Because Eternity will last,
When life, and even death, are past.

LVI.

UPON DEATH.

WHERE should I be, if God should say
I must not live another day,
And send to take away my breath?
—What is Eternity—and Death?

My body is of little worth;
'Twould soon be mingled with the earth:
We all were form'd of clay at first,
And shall return again to dust:

But where my living soul would go,
I do not, and I cannot know;
For none were e'er sent back to tell
The joys of heav'n, or pains of hell.

Yet heav'n must be a world of bliss,
Where GOD himself for ever is;
Where saints around his throne adore,
And never sin nor suffer more.

And hell's a state of endless woe,
Where unrepenting sinners go;—
Though none that seek the SAVIOUR's grace
Shall ever see that dreadful place.

O let me, then, at once apply
To Him, who did for sinners die!
And this shall be my great reward,
To dwell for ever with the Lord.

LVII.

AGAINST SELFISHNESS.

Love and kindness we may measure
  By this simple rule alone:
Do we mind our neighbour's pleasure,
  Just as if it were our own?

Let us try to care for others,
  Nor suppose ourselves the best:
We should all be friends and brothers—
  'Twas the Saviour's last request.

His example we should borrow,
  Who forsook his throne above,
And endur'd such pain and sorrow,
  Out of tenderness and love.

When the poor are unbefriended,
  When we will not pity lend,
Christ accounts himself offended,
  Who is ev'ry creature's friend.

Let us not be so ungrateful,
  Thus his goodness to reward ;
Selfishness, indeed, is hateful
  In the followers of the Lord.

When a selfish thought would seize us,
  And our resolution break,
Let us then remember JESUS,
  And resist it for his sake.

LVIII.

"IN THE MORNING IT FLOURISHETH AND GROW-
ETH UP; IN THE EVENING IT IS CUT DOWN
AND WITHERETH."

THE flowers of the field,
  That quickly fade away,
May well to us instruction yield,
  Who die as soon as they.

That pretty rosebud see,
  Decaying on the walk;
A storm came sweeping o'er the tree,
  And broke its feeble stalk.

Just like an early rose,
  I've seen an infant bloom;
But Death, perhaps, before it blows,
  Will lay it in the tomb.

Then let us think on death,
  Though we are young and gay;
For God, who gave our life and breath,
  Can take them soon away.

To God, who loves them all,
  Let children humbly cry;
And then, whenever Death may call,
  They'll be prepar'd to die.

LIX.

HUMILITY.

In a modest, humble mind
  God himself will take delight;
But the proud and haughty find
  They are hateful in his sight.

Jesus Christ was meek and mild,
　And no angry thoughts allow'd :
O, then, shall a little child
　Dare to be perverse and proud!

This, indeed should never be ;—
　Lord, forbid it, we entreat ;
Grant they all may learn of thee,
　That humility is sweet :

Make it shine in ev'ry part ;
　Fill them with this heav'nly grace ;
For a little infant's heart
　Surely is its proper place.

LX.

"SET YOUR AFFECTIONS ON THINGS ABOVE."

Why should our poor enjoyments here
Be thought so pleasant and so dear,
　And tempt our hearts astray ?
Our brightest joys are fading fast,
The longest life will soon be past ;
And if we go to heav'n at last,
　We need not wish to stay.

85.

For when we come to dwell above,
Where all is holiness and love,
   And endless pleasures flow,
Our threescore years and ten will seem
Just like a short and busy dream;
And O, how poor we then shall deem
   Our best pursuits below!

Perhaps the happy saints in bliss
Look down from their bright world to this,
   Where once they used to dwell;
And wonder why we trifle so,
And love these vanities below,
And live as if we did not know
   There was a heav'n and hell.

LXI.

FOR THE LAST DAY OF THE YEAR.

This year is just going away,
   The moments are finishing fast:
My heart, have you nothing to say
   Concerning the time that is past?

Now, while in my chamber alone,
   Where God will be present to hear,
I'll try to remember, and own,
   The faults I've committed this year.

O Lord, I'm asham'd to confess
   How often I've broken thy day!
Perhaps I have thought of my dress,
   Or wasted the moments in play;
And when the good minister tried
   To make little children attend,
I was thinking of something beside,
   Or wishing the sermon would end!

How often I rose from my bed,
   And did not remember my pray'r;
Or if a few words I have said,
   My thoughts have been going elsewhere!
Ill temper, and passion, and pride,
   Have griev'd my dear parents, and thee;
And seldom I've heartily tried
   Obedient and gentle to be!

But, Lord, thou already hast known
   Much more of my folly than I;

There is not a fault I can own,
   Too little for GOD to descry:
Yet hear me, and help me to feel
   How wicked and weak I must be;
And let me not try to conceal
   The largest, or smallest, from thee.

This year is just going away,
   The moments are finishing fast:
Look down, in thy mercy, I pray,
   To pardon the time that is past:
And as soon as another begins,
   So help me to walk in thy fear,
That I may not with follies and sins
   Disfigure and waste a new year.

LXII.

THE LILY OF THE VALLEY.

COME, my love, and do not spurn
From a little flow'r to learn.—
See the lily on the bed,
Hanging down its modest head;

While it scarcely can be seen,
Folded in its leaf of green :

Yet we love the lily well,
For its sweet and pleasant smell ;
And would rather call it ours,
Than a many gayer flow'rs :
Pretty lilies seem to be
Emblems of humility.

Come, my love, and do not spurn
From a little flow'r to learn :—
Let your temper be as sweet
As the lily at your feet :
Be as gentle, be as mild ;
Be a modest, simple child.

'Tis not beauty that we prize—
Like a summer flow'r it dies ;
But humility will last,
Fair and sweet, when beauty's past:
And the Saviour from above
Views a humble child with love.

LXIII.

"THEN THE LORD CALLED SAMUEL, AND SAMUEL
SAID, SPEAK, FOR THY SERVANT HEARETH."

WHEN little Samuel woke,
 And heard his MAKER's voice,
At ev'ry word He spoke,
 How much did he rejoice:
O blessed, happy child, to find
The God of heav'n so near and kind!

If GOD would speak to me,
 And say He was my friend,
How happy *I* should be!
 O how would I attend!
The smallest sin I then should fear,
If GOD ALMIGHTY were so near.

And does he never speak?——
 O yes; for in his word
He bids me come and seek
 The GOD that Samuel heard:

In almost ev'ry page I see,
The God of Samuel calls to me.

And I beneath his care
    May safely rest my head;
I know that God is there,
    To guard my humble bed:
And ev'ry sin I well may fear,
Since God Almighty *is* so near.

Like Samuel, let me say,
    Whene'er I read his word,
" Speak, Lord; I would obey
    " The voice that *I* have heard:
" And when I in thy house appear,
" Speak, for thy servant waits to hear."

LXIV.

ON REPEATING THE CATECHISM.

As Mary sat at Jesus' feet,
    To learn her Maker's will,
We in the Saviour's presence meet,
    And hear his doctrine still.

Still he beholds the wand'ring look,
  Each foolish thought discerns;
And knows who idles at his book,
  And who in earnest learns.

O for that meek, attentive mind,
  Which happy Mary show'd;
And that instruction may we find,
  That was on her bestow'd.

Here we are taught the sacred word
  The Saviour first convey'd;
And here the doctrines we have heard
  Are plain and easy made.

'Tis here we learn the glorious name
  Of God, who reigns above;
And while we read of sinners' shame,
  Are taught the Saviour's love.

Lord! while we thank thee for the grace
  That sends this happy news,
We still would sit in Mary's place,
  Her better part to choose.

LXV.

BROTHERLY LOVE.

The God of heav'n is pleas'd to see
A little family agree;
And will not slight the praise they bring,
When loving children join to sing.

For love and kindness please him more
Than if we gave him all our store;
And children here, who dwell in love,
Are like his happy ones above.

The gentle child, that tries to please;
That hates to quarrel, fret, and teaze;
And would not say an angry word:
That child is pleasing to the Lord.

Great God! forgive, whenever we
Forget thy will, and disagree;
And grant that each of us may find
The sweet delight of being kind.

LXVI.

THE CONDESCENSION OF GOD.

God!—what a great and awful word!
  O who can speak his worth!
By saints in heav'n he is ador'd,
  And fear'd by men on earth;
And yet a little child may bend,
And say, My Father and my Friend!

The glorious sun, that blazes high;
  The moon, more pale and dim;
And all the stars that fill the sky,
  Are made and rul'd by him;
And yet a child may ask his care,
'And call upon his name in pray'r!

And this large world of ours below,
  The waters and the land,
With all the trees and flow'rs that grow,
  Were fashion'd by his hand;

Yes, and he forms our infant race,—
And even I may seek his grace !

Ten thousand angels sing his praise
   On high, to harps of gold ;
But holy angels dare not gaze,
   His brightness to behold ;
Yet a poor lowly infant may
Lift up its voice to God, and pray !

The saints in heav'n before him fall,
   And round his throne appear;
Adam, and Abraham, and all
   Who lov'd and serv'd him here ;
And I, a child on earth, may raise
My feeble voice in humble praise.

And all his faithful servants now,
   The wise, and good, and just,
Before his sacred footstool bow,
   And own they are but dust ;
But what can I presume to say ?
Yet he will listen when I pray !

O yes; when little children cry,
   He hearkens to their pray'r;
His throne of grace is always nigh,
   And I will venture there;
I'll go, depending on his word,
And seek his grace, through CHRIST the Lord.

LXVII.

THE CHILD OF AFFLUENCE.

How many poor indigent children I see,
Who want all the comforts bestow'd upon me!
But though I'm preserv'd from such want and dis-
     tress,
I'm quite as unworthy of all I possess.

While I am partaking a plentiful meal,
How many the cravings of appetite feel!
Poor children, as young and as helpless as I,
Who yet have no money their wants to supply!

If I were so destitute, friendless, and poor,
How could I such hardship and suff'ring endure!

Then let me be thankful, and humbly adore
My GOD, who has graciously given me more.

And since I with so many comforts am blest,
May it be my delight to relieve the distrest;
For GOD has declar'd, and his promise is sure,
That blessed are they who consider the poor.

LXVIII.

THE CHILD OF POVERTY.

LORD, I am poor; yet hear my call;
   Afford me daily bread;
Give me at least the crumbs that fall
   From tables richly spread.

Thou canst for all my wants provide,
   And bless my homely crust:
The ravens cry, and are supply'd,
   And ought not I to trust?

Behold the lilies, how they grow,
   Though they can nothing do;
And will not GOD, who clothes them so,
   Afford me raiment too?

But seeing, Lord, thou dost withhold
   The riches some possess,
Grant me, what better is than gold,
   Thy grace and righteousness.

O may I heav'nly treasures find,
   And choose the better part;
Give me a humble, pious mind,
   A meek and lowly heart.

Forgive my sins, my follies cure,
   And grant the grace I need;
And then, though I am mean and poor,
   I shall be rich indeed.

LXIX.

PRAISE TO GOD.

ALMIGHTY GOD, who dwellest high,
   Where mortals cannot gaze,
If thou wilt listen, I will try
   To sing a hymn of praise.

G

Angels adore thee, and rejoice—
  Such praise to thee belongs;
But wilt thou hear a feeble voice,
  Amid their lofty songs?

My thoughts are vain, my heart is hard,
  And poor the thanks I pay;
O how unworthy thy regard
  Is all that I can say!

My feeble pow'rs can never rise
  To praise thee as I ought;
For thou art great, and good, and wise,
  Beyond my highest thought.

The happy souls who dwell on high
  Can tell thy glories best;
And may I enter, when I die,
  The mansions of the blest!

There we shall better praises bring,
  And raise our voices higher,
Angels will teach us how to sing,
  And we shall never tire.

LXX.

HEAVEN AND EARTH.

Come, let us now forget our mirth,
   And think that we must die:
What are our best delights on earth,
   Compar'd with those on high?

A sad and sinful world is this,
   Although it seems so fair;
But heav'n is perfect joy and bliss,
   For God himself is there.

Here all our pleasures soon are past,
   Our brightest joys decay;
But pleasures there for ever last,
   And cannot fade away.

Here many a pain, and bitter groan,
   Our feeble bodies tear;
But pain and sickness are not known,
   And never shall be, there.

Here sins and sorrows we deplore,
 With many cares distrest,
But there the mourners weep no more,
 And there the weary rest.

Our dearest friends, when death shall call,
 At once must hence depart;
But there we hope to meet them all,
 And never, never part.

Then let us love and serve the Lord
 With all our youthful pow'rs,
And we shall gain this great reward,
 This glory shall be ours.

Printed by G. Ellerton, Johnson Court, Fleet Street London

www.ingramcontent.com/pod-product-compliance
Lightning Source LLC
LaVergne TN
LVHW061219060426
835508LV00014B/1360